# Honky-Tonk Heroes & Hillbilly Angels

## The Pioneers of Country & Western Music

Words by HOLLY GEORGE-WARREN

Pictures by LAURA LEVINE

HOUGHTON MIFFLIN COMPANY BOSTON 2006

To my parents, Martha and Alvis,
who taught me to love music,
and my brothers, Owen and Robert,
who learned to love it with me. —H.G-W.

For Katherine, Nicholas,
Anna, Leo, and Veronika,
with love. —L.L.

# ≋ INTRODUCTION ≋

Before the invention of records, radio, movies, and television, people entertained themselves by playing instruments and singing. In the 1800s, emigrants to America brought with them old folk songs. Many of these settlers homesteaded in the hills of the Carolinas, Georgia, Virginia, Kentucky, and Tennessee. There, the mountaineers played fiddles, banjos, and guitars. Singers crooned ballads about such calamities as murders and train wrecks. The best musicians competed at local fiddling contests, and young and old kicked up their heels at Saturday night hoedowns called barn dances.

In the 1920s, northern talent scouts ventured into the backwoods to record the music they named "hillbilly." They released it on records, and soon radio helped to spread the music too. In 1924, a Chicago station first broadcast a professional barn dance program featuring comedians, musicians, and entertainers yodeling cowboy songs. Those tunes became very popular, and some artists began dressing up as cowboys and cowgirls— even if they didn't know one end of a horse from the other. The next year, a Nashville radio station started its own Saturday night barn dance program. Making fun of hoity-toity audiences who listened to grand opera, the show's MC, George D. Hay, called his program the Grand Ole Opry. Because of the music's rural and cowboy style, people began to call it "country & western," or "C&W."

Out west, in the 1940s, C&W got louder in roadhouses and saloons called honky-tonks. Because people danced and acted rowdy in these places, the musicians plugged their guitars into amplifiers and added drums to be heard over the din. Vocalists sang about whiskey, broken marriages, and other tragedies of modern life. Large honky-tonk bands included horn sections and called their style "Western swing." In the 1950s, some musicians mixed country & western with the blues, giving birth to rock & roll. C&W grew more polished and gradually lost its rural flavor and twanginess, and the music's name got shortened to "country." Today's country stars would not exist without the pioneers who created a truly American sound: country & western music.

# THE CARTER FAMILY

## MAYBELLE CARTER (1909·1978)
## SARA CARTER (1898·1979)
## A. P. CARTER (1891·1960)

The Carter Family was country music's first famous group. They turned 100-year-old folk ballads, old-timey parlor songs, gospel music, and blues tunes into hit records. Many of the Carters' 350 songs, including "Will the Circle Be Unbroken," have become American music standards.

Living in the mountains of Virginia, the Carter Family included A. P. (Alvin Pleasant) Carter, his wife, Sara Dougherty Carter, and Sara's cousin Maybelle Addington Carter. Each had grown up playing music, Sara on autoharp, A.P. on fiddle, and Maybelle on guitar.

In 1927, the Carter Family auditioned in Bristol, Tennessee, for Victor Records talent scout Ralph Peer. Mr. Peer loved what he heard: Sara sang lead with her rich, mournful alto voice and strummed the guitar or autoharp. Maybelle accompanied her with an intricate guitar-picking style and emotive tenor vocals. A.P. joined in, singing bass. The trio's unique harmonizing convinced Mr. Peer to give the Carters a record deal. Carter Family hits included "Keep on the Sunny Side," an 1899 Sunday school number that became their theme song, and "Wildwood Flower," which dated back to the Civil War and showcased Maybelle's innovative guitar-picking. Known as the Carter Scratch, her technique helped to turn the guitar into a lead instrument and influenced several generations of pickers. Eventually, Sara and A.P. divorced, and the group split up in 1943. A.P. ran a country store, Sara moved to California, and Maybelle started an act called Mother Maybelle and the Carter Sisters, featuring her daughters, June, Helen, and Anita. June later married country star Johnny Cash, who invited his wife and her mother and sisters to join him in his traveling show and on his records. Maybelle and Sara briefly reunited at folk and bluegrass festivals in the 1960s, and their music became popular once again.

THE CARTER FAMILY

SARA

MAYBELLE
THE
FIRST FAMILY OF COUNTRY MUSIC

LAURA LEVINE

# JIMMIE RODGERS
## (1897 · 1933)

Jimmie Rodgers was the first "hillbilly" superstar. When he began his singing career, he was working on the railroad to make ends meet, and he became known as "The Singing Brakeman" because he wore his work duds — a train engineer's overalls and cap — while performing. Jimmie wrote and recorded many popular songs, but what really wowed the crowds was the way he yodeled. A kind of high-pitched, hiccupping singing style first heard in the Swiss Alps, yodeling added a bluesy flavor to Jimmie's music.

As a kid growing up in Mississippi, Jimmie performed on the streets and sometimes traveled with tent shows. Working on the railroad, he listened to the blues sung by his black coworkers and by the hoboes who rode the rails. Jimmie blended their music with folk songs, old-fashioned ballads, and a touch of New Orleans jazz, creating his own catchy style. In 1927, Jimmie quit the railroad after contracting tuberculosis, or TB, but he couldn't stop playing the music he loved. He started a band and got a show on a North Carolina radio station. Like the Carter Family, he heard about a Victor Records audition in nearby Bristol. On the way there, his group argued and broke up. His haphazard solo tryout resulted in a contract, though, and hit records soon followed. These included "In the Jailhouse Now," "Muleskinner Blues," "Peach Pickin' Time in Georgia," "TB Blues," and "Blue Yodel #9," which gave him yet another nickname, "the Blue Yodeler." Future entertainers such as Bill Monroe and Webb Pierce would later cover his songs, turning them into hits once again.

Though his health worsened, Jimmie continued to perform. While making a new record in New York City in 1933, he got so sick he had to lie down between songs. He decided to take a break to relax at Coney Island, but he collapsed on the way and died. His heartbroken fans gathered along the railroad tracks all the way from New York to Mississippi to pay respect to the funeral train bearing his body home.

Only thirty-six at his death, Jimmie Rodgers forever changed the course of popular music. Combining black and white styles, he created a new sound that would influence many country & western artists, as well as a future genre called rock & roll.

# ROY ACUFF

## (1903 · 1992)

As a boy, Roy Acuff thought he would grow up to be a baseball player, never dreaming he'd turn out to be an entertainer. Born in Tennessee's Smoky Mountains, Roy loved sports as a child. His skill on the ball field landed him in the semipros, but in 1929 he suffered the first of several sunstrokes. He realized he had to take up another career, and luckily his next-door neighbor invited him to join his medicine show as an entertainer. Helping to sell a "cure-all" called Moc-a-Tan, Roy acted in skits, sometimes dressing like a little girl or an old lady. He also played the fiddle and sang folk songs he'd known since childhood.

At age thirty, Roy formed his first band, the Tennessee Crackerjacks. They played on radio programs and began winning fans with their string-band music and hymns. After changing their name to the Crazy Tennesseans, they auditioned for the Grand Ole Opry in 1936. Roy first sang a song about a rooster in his high tenor voice, then launched into an eerie old gospel number, "The Great Speckle Bird," and brought the house down. Because of their immediate popularity, Roy and his group were invited by the Opry to become regulars on the show.

Renamed the Smoky Mountain Boys, Roy and his band scored numerous hits, including "Wreck on the Highway," "Hillbilly Fever," and a remake of the Carter Family's "Wabash Cannonball." Roy and his boys were beloved for their traditional mountain songs and rambunctious entertaining. Some of Roy's tricks included yo-yo spinning, balancing his fiddle bow on his nose, and making the authentic sound of a train whistle. Baseball legend Dizzy Dean gave him the nickname "King of the Hillbillies," which later became "King of Country Music."

As an old man, Roy moved out of his mansion and into a little house on the grounds of Opryland, where the Grand Ole Opry had moved from downtown Nashville. He lived there and performed on the Opry nearly every weekend until his death at the age of eighty-nine.

# GENE AUTRY
## (1907 · 1998)

America's most successful singing cowboy, Gene Autry brought the words, music, and look of Western cowpokes to country music. Gene started singing in public at age five in his grandfather's country church, and soon his mother taught him to play guitar. Working as a shoeshine boy at Sam's Barbershop in Tioga, Texas, he endeared himself to customers, who made him a guitar by attaching some wire to a wooden cigar box. When Gene was twelve, he'd saved enough money to order a real instrument from the Sears catalogue. At seventeen, he landed a job as a railroad telegraph operator. One night while working in an Oklahoma train depot, he met entertainer Will Rogers. Hearing Gene sing and play guitar, Will encouraged him to give showbiz a try. Gene soon landed a spot on a local radio station, billed as "The Oklahoma Yodeling Cowboy." He cowrote songs with a railroad buddy named Jimmy Long and took them to record companies in New York. Their song "That Silver Haired Daddy of Mine" became the first-ever gold record and got Gene on Chicago's National

Barn Dance.

In 1934, Gene went to Hollywood and began starring in musical cowboy movies. Starting with *Tumbling Tumbleweeds*, Gene played himself — a singing, guitar-playing hero who defeated the bad guys. Gene got help from his supersmart horse, Champion. The movies' songs became hits, including his theme song, "Back in the Saddle Again." Gene's colorful buckaroo outfits began influencing country artists, who also started wearing cowboy shirts, hats, and boots.

Gene's biggest fans were kids, so he started singing special holiday songs just for them, including "Here Comes Santa Claus" and "Rudolph the Red-Nosed Reindeer." After he retired from entertaining, Gene bought a baseball team, the California Angels. In 2002, four years after Gene's death at age ninety-one, his team won the World Series for the first time. People in the stadium shouted, "They won it for the Cowboy!" and sang his famous words, "I'm back in the saddle again."

# ERNEST TUBB

## (1914 · 1984)

Ernest Tubb began his career as a Jimmie Rodgers copycat before creating his own brand of honky-tonk music. He grew up on a small cotton farm near the tiny town of Crisp, Texas. Rather than work in the fields like his brothers and sisters, Ernest decided to become an entertainer. After Jimmie Rodgers's death in 1933, Ernest wanted everyone to remember his hero's music, so he started singing the Blue Yodeler's songs on the radio. One day Jimmie's widow, Carrie, heard Ernest and liked his music so much that she offered to help make him a star. She gave him her husband's prized Martin guitar and helped boost his career by introducing him to people in the music business.

Eventually, though, Ernest had to develop his own style after his tonsils were removed and his voice was no longer high like Jimmie's. His new bass singing impressed lots of people, and he started writing songs to suit it. He hired a top-notch honky-tonk band and named them the Texas Troubadours. The group featured a superb electric guitarist named Billy Byrd. Before this time, most country artists used acoustic guitar. One of Tubb's original songs, "Walking the Floor Over You," became his first smash in 1941.

Ernest, who got the nickname E.T., toured the country for four decades. His crowd-pleasers included "Waltz Across Texas" and "Slippin' Around." E.T. also scored hit duets with the Andrews Sisters, the Wilburn Brothers, Red Foley, and Loretta Lynn. He was so popular that he became the first country artist invited to perform at New York's prestigious Carnegie Hall. He preferred playing on the Grand Ole Opry, though, and he did so almost every

Saturday night. Noticing that Opry fans wanted a nearby place to buy records, he opened the Ernest Tubb Record Shop. Following the Opry performance, everyone would head over to the record shop for Tubb's Midnite Jamboree, where new artists could perform and be heard over the radio. Many famous entertainers got discovered this way. Though E.T. died in 1984, his legacy lives on at the Midnite Jamboree, which is still going strong every Saturday night.

A native of Kentucky, Bill Monroe helped to create the bluegrass sound by combining several musical styles he loved — string-band music, the blues, and gospel. In the 1940s, he formed the Blue Grass Boys — named after his home state's nickname — and the group continued to play until his death more than fifty years later.

Bill grew up the youngest of a large musical family. His mother and his Uncle Pen were both fine fiddle players, and his brothers liked to sing and play guitar. Bill took up the mandolin and also learned the blues from a black guitarist named Arnold Schultz, who yodeled like Jimmie Rodgers. After his parents died, Bill traveled to Chicago to join two of his brothers, Charlie and Birch, who had moved there to find work. The three of them started a musical group called the Monroe Brothers. After Birch quit, it became a duo. Charlie sang lead and played guitar, and Bill crooned the high harmonies and picked the mandolin. They got sponsorship from a company called Crazy Water Crystals, which paid for them to tour the country and promote its product between songs. Bill and Charlie squabbled, and they eventually broke up. After first forming a similar-sounding group called the Kentuckians, Bill put together the Blue Grass Boys, which included such instruments as the fiddle and upright bass. In 1945, North Carolina–born Earl Scruggs added his superb banjo playing to Bill's musical mix. Earl sounded great with the rhythmic strumming of guitarist Lester Flatt, fiddler Chubby Wise, and bassist Cedric Rainwater. This five-piece version of the Blue Grass Boys perfected Bill's unique bluegrass style. Bill began writing songs that have become classics, such as "The Kentucky Waltz," "Uncle Pen," and "Blue Moon of Kentucky." He also adapted a Jimmie Rodgers yodel into a song he called "Muleskinner Blues."

After a couple of years, Lester and Earl left to form their own group, Flatt and Scruggs and the Foggy Mountain Boys. Their catchy song "The Ballad of Jed Clampett" was the first bluegrass record to hit number one. Meanwhile, Bill continued to perform, breaking in new band members almost every year, giving many players their start. He kept up a busy pace well into his eighties, and died in 1996 after suffering a stroke.

Bandleader, fiddler, and songwriter Bob Wills was one of the first artists to play dance music that combined country & western, blues, jazz, pop, and swing. His group, the Texas Playboys, which at times had eighteen members, included horns, fiddles, electric guitar, upright bass, piano, banjo, drums, and a lead singer.

He was born James Robert Wills (and nicknamed Jim Rob), the oldest son of a fiddler who led his ten kids across Texas in search of a better life. The family picked cotton as migrants, and young Jim Rob heard the blues sung by fellow workers. By age ten, Jim Rob had mastered the fiddle well enough to entertain at square dances. As a teenager, he joined a medicine show, where he met vocalist Milton Brown. The two formed a duo, which soon expanded into a group called Aladdin's Laddies. When the Light Crust Flour Company became the sponsor of their radio show in 1931, they changed the name to the Light Crust Doughboys. Their music also changed from old-timey country to danceable country swing.

Using the name Bob Wills, he eventually split off from Milton and started his own group called the Playboys, which included his brother Johnny Lee on banjo and vocalist Tommy Duncan. When they moved to Oklahoma, he added "Texas" to his group's name and hired several new members, including steel guitarist Leon McAuliffe. Bob's songs "New San Antonio Rose," "Roly Poly," and "Faded Love" became huge hits, and the group was billed as "the Most Versatile Band in the World" at large halls across America. After World War II, Bob moved with the Texas Playboys to California, where they continued to keep the dance floors hoppin' with such standards as "Take Me Back to Tulsa" and "Steel Guitar Rag." Though Bob died over thirty years ago, his Western swing has remained popular in dance halls. A new generation of artists — like Asleep at the Wheel — has taken up Western swing, keeping the sound alive and winning Grammy awards in the process.

LAURA LEVINE 2004

# KITTY WELLS

## (b. 1919)

Kitty Wells became the first woman to reach number one on the country charts. Her success inspired more women to become country artists and persuaded the record labels and radio stations to give them a chance.

Kitty was born Muriel Deason in Nashville and began playing guitar and singing as a young girl. At fifteen, she met Johnny Wright, a budding hillbilly singer/songwriter, and they married two years later. The couple started a group with songwriter Jack Anglin and began zigzagging the South, hosting shows at a string of radio stations. During a Knoxville, Tennessee, stint, the program director encouraged Mrs. Wright to adopt a catchier stage name. Johnny suggested "Kitty Wells" — the name of his favorite folk song — and from then on it was "Johnny and Jack Featuring Kitty Wells." To look the part of the character in the song, Kitty sometimes wore a long calico dress and an old-fashioned bonnet. Kitty had almost decided to give up touring and stay home with her three children when,

practically overnight, she became one of country's biggest stars. It happened when Johnny found an "answer song" for Kitty to record called "It Wasn't God Who Made Honky-Tonk Angels." It was the response to a Hank Thompson hit, "The Wild Side of Life," that pointed the finger at wayward wives for breaking up marriages. Kitty's song took the women's side and blamed unfaithful husbands for causing their wives to stray. This was the first time such a viewpoint had been expressed in a song, and it took the nation by storm, reaching the top of the charts in 1952.

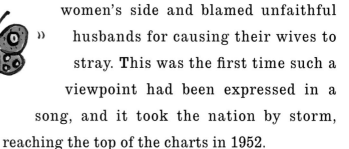

After Kitty's success, more labels signed female singers and more songwriters wrote from a woman's point of view. Over the next three decades, Kitty scored seventy-eight hits, including "Paying for That Back Street Affair," "Makin' Believe," "Hey Joe," "Release Me," and "Mommy for a Day." Kitty, along with her husband and children, continued to tour the world until her retirement in 2003.

The greatest country artist of all time, Alabama-born Hiram "Hank" King Williams lived to be only twenty-nine years old. During his short and tumultuous life, he wrote numerous classics, became a hit-making sensation, spread C&W to a national audience, and influenced several generations of singers and songwriters.

Throughout most of Hank's childhood, his father was confined to a hospital. To support the family, his mother ran a boarding-house and roasted peanuts for Hank to sell on the streets of their small town. There, he met an elderly blues singer, Rufus "Tee-Tot" Payne, who taught eleven-year-old Hank some guitar riffs. By the time he reached his teens, Hank was playing to schoolhouse audiences by day and in honky-tonks by night. When the Williamses moved to Montgomery in 1937, Hank started performing on the radio, billed as "the Singing Kid."

While appearing in a medicine show one summer, Hank met and married a lovely blonde named Audrey. Hank formed a group called the Drifting Cowboys and started writing songs, many of them inspired by arguments with his wife. He went to Nashville, where he met Fred Rose, who helped with his writing and got him a record contract. Soon after, he scored his first enormous smash, "Lovesick Blues," and joined the Grand Ole Opry. His "Cold, Cold Heart," "Hey, Good Lookin'," and "Your Cheatin' Heart" were the first country songs to become big hits on the pop charts after being covered by such crooners as Tony Bennett and Jo Stafford.

Sadly, over the years Hank had developed a dependence on alcohol and an addiction to painkillers. He had severe back problems, his health deteriorated, and he began missing shows. The Grand Ole Opry fired him, and Audrey divorced him. Though he was a broken man, he still tried to perform. Just after the release of his single "I'll Never Get Out of This World Alive," Hank died of heart failure on the way to a New Year's concert. Today, his music is as popular as ever, and following in his musical footsteps are his son, Hank Jr., his daughter, Jett, and his grandchildren Hank III and Holly.

With her robust voice and impressive range, Patsy Cline became one of country's first artists to strike gold on the pop charts. She pioneered the Nashville Sound, a polished C&W style that used small orchestras and background singers to "sweeten" the sound.

Patsy was born Virginia Hensley in Winchester, Virginia. After her father deserted the family, fifteen-year-old Virginia helped out by getting a job in a drugstore. She also began fronting local country bands, wearing a cowboy hat and boots and a cowgirl outfit her mom made her. She loved to yodel, and her boisterous stage presence made her a real crowd pleaser. After she wed a man named Gerald Cline, she changed her name to Patsy Cline. Though most married women of the day stayed home and kept house, Patsy continued to sing in nightclubs and appeared on local television programs. Her marriage broke up, but she got a recording contract with a small record label. "Walkin' After Midnight" became her first smash in 1957. Four years later she moved to powerful Decca Records. There, the famous producer Owen Bradley took her under his wing and directed her to some of Nashville's best musicians. Patsy sought out material by such talented young songwriters as Harlan Howard, Hank Cochran, and a then-unknown named Willie Nelson, who would become a big star himself in the 1970s. Howard and Cochran's "I Fall to Pieces" became her first number one. An even bigger hit was Nelson's "Crazy," followed by "Sweet Dreams (of You)" and a version of Bob Wills's "Faded Love." Patsy became a popular guest on national TV shows and was one of the first country artists to perform in Las Vegas and at Carnegie Hall.

Tragically, Patsy's career was cut short when she was killed in a plane crash along with her manager and recording artists Cowboy Copas and Hawkshaw Hawkins. Over the years, her music has become more popular than ever, and her life has been the subject of a 1985 movie and two musicals. She remains one of the top-selling female artists of all time.

# BUCK OWENS

## (b. 1929)

Buck Owens became a hotshot guitar player in Bakersfield, California, before finding stardom as a singer, songwriter, and bandleader. His high-octane music helped to create what's called the Bakersfield Sound, a more rockin' style of C&W.

Born Alvis Edgar Owens in Sherman, Texas, Buck was surrounded by music as a child. His mother played piano in church, his father blew harmonica and sang, and his two uncles picked guitars. The family listened to the Grand Ole Opry every Saturday night, and four-year-old Buck thought little people lived inside the radio and played the music. Buck's sharecropping family migrated to Mesa, Arizona, and when he reached his teens he played guitar in honky-tonks. He married an aspiring singer named Bonnie, and the couple moved to California in 1949. In Bakersfield, he got work at a honky-tonk called the Blackboard as lead guitarist of its house band, the Schoolhouse Playboys. Buck developed a unique style on his electric Telecaster guitar and became the band's front man and lead singer. He also played on records in nearby Los Angeles by such artists as the rockabilly queen Wanda Jackson.

In the early 1960s, Buck formed his own group, the Buckaroos, which featured a young Washington State native named Don Rich on harmony vocals and guitar. Beginning in 1963, the band hit the jackpot on the country charts, with "Act Naturally," followed by "Together Again," "Tiger by the Tail," and many other songs. The Bakersfield Sound became very popular, and among its stars was his now ex-wife Bonnie's second husband, Merle Haggard, whose band the Strangers included Bonnie on harmony vocals. Buck also starred in the popular country TV show *Hee-Haw*. He replaced his fancy rhinestoned suits with overalls to pop out of a cornfield with cohost Roy Clark. In 1988, country star Dwight Yoakam brought Buck and his hometown style back into the limelight when they recorded the duet "Streets of Bakersfield," which soared to number one. Today Buck and the Buckaroos play every weekend at his Bakersfield nightclub, the Crystal Palace.

# ( b. 1935 )

Loretta Lynn was the first woman solo artist in country music to focus on writing her own hit songs. Born Loretta Webb, the daughter of a Butcher Hollow, Kentucky, coal miner, she was named after her mother's favorite movie star, Loretta Young. One of eight kids, Loretta loved to sing to her brothers and sisters. When she was thirteen, she met Mooney "Doolittle" Lynn, who'd just returned to Butcher Hollow following a stint in the service. "Doo" swept Loretta off her feet, and the two married. They moved to Custer, Washington, and by the time she was eighteen, Loretta had four children.

In 1953, Doo bought Loretta a guitar, and with his encouragement she began writing songs and performing. One of her compositions, "Honky Tonk Girl," inspired by Kitty Wells, was released by a local label. Loretta and her husband traveled the country, stopping at radio stations and asking DJs to play her single. The disc jockeys loved Loretta's voice and charm, and eventually her record became a hit. In Nashville, Ernest Tubb invited Loretta to sing at his Midnite Jamboree, which led to a spot on the Grand Ole Opry and a record deal. Before long, Loretta had a national hit with 1966's "Don't Come Home a Drinkin'," her first number one. The feisty Loretta really spoke her mind in such songs as "Your Squaw's on the Warpath" and "Fist City," telling gals to stand up for their rights. Loretta scored seventy top-twenty C&W hits and sixteen number ones, several with duet partners Ernest Tubb and Conway Twitty.

One of her hits, "Coal Miner's Daughter," described Loretta's childhood, and it later became the title of her autobiography, which was turned into a popular movie starring Sissy Spacek. By the late 1960s, Loretta was headlining concert tours, a first for women in country music, and in 1972 she became the first woman named Entertainer of the Year by the Country Music Association. Today, the spunky Loretta still records and performs, most recently working with Jack White, of the rock group White Stripes.

# TAMMY WYNETTE

## (1942 · 1998)

 Two of the greatest vocalists in country music, George Jones and Tammy Wynette, each had long solo careers. In the late 1960s they began singing duets together and became even more popular as a couple.

George Jones was born in Saratoga, Texas, and grew up in nearby Beaumont. As a boy, he started singing and playing guitar on the sidewalks of town. He loved his guitar so much, he always carried it with him, even to school, hiding it in the woods before going inside. George began playing professionally while in the army. In the 1950s, he started recording hits, such as "Why, Baby, Why," "White Lightning," and "Who Shot Sam." He enjoyed singing duets and scored some smashes with Melba Montgomery, including the song "We Must Have Been Out of Our Minds."

Meanwhile, Tammy Wynette was singing on an early-bird **TV** show before rushing off to work at a beauty shop in Birmingham, Alabama. Born Wynette Pugh in Red Bay, Alabama, she toiled in her grandparents' cotton fields in rural Mississippi as a girl. She married at sixteen, had three children, and then

TAMMY WYNETTE

THE KING AND QUE

# GEORGE JONES
## (b. 1931)

GEORGE JONES

GEORGE

N of BROKEN HEARTS

LAURA LEVINE 2005

divorced her husband and moved from Alabama to Nashville in 1966. She auditioned for a producer named Billy Sherrill, and her full, dramatic voice bowled him over. He gave her the more glamorous name Tammy Wynette, and together they began recording such heartbreaking songs as "Apartment #9," "D-I-V-O-R-C-E," "I Don't Wanna Play House," and her most famous, "Stand by Your Man," which she cowrote.

In the late 1960s, she began performing with George Jones, and the pair fell in love. They chronicled the happy days of their marriage in the duets "(We're Not) the Jet Set" and "The Ceremony." George's heavy drinking and the stress of their hectic lifestyles took a toll on their relationship, though. The couple divorced in 1975 and went their separate ways. Eventually they let bygones be bygones and occasionally recorded more duets, reuniting for the last time in 1995. Three years later, Tammy died in her sleep after years of health problems. George has carried on and is considered country's greatest living vocalist.

A successful recording artist for nearly fifty years, Johnny Cash was blessed with a distinctive deep voice, a talent for writing powerful original songs, and a charismatic personality that made him one of America's greatest and most popular entertainers.

As a young boy in rural Arkansas, Cash listened to blues music and to the Grand Ole Opry on the radio. He also sang gospel songs in church. After high school, he joined the air force and began playing guitar and writing songs while he was stationed in Germany. After his discharge in 1954, he moved to Memphis, where he began his career as a rockabilly artist with his band the Tennessee Two. Some of his first songwriting efforts — "Cry, Cry, Cry," "I Walk the Line," and "Folsom Prison Blues" — became huge hits. Over the years, his songs took on a more country flavor, but throughout the 1960s he would also sing folk, rhythm & blues, gospel, and pop songs. He spoke out for the down-trodden, including prison inmates and Native Americans, and he began dressing in black to protest injustices. The live recording of Johnny's 1968 Folsom Prison concert became a smash. It included the hit "A Boy Named Sue," a novelty number written by Shel Silverstein. Johnny toured constantly, along with his second wife, June Carter Cash, her family, and their son, John Carter. Johnny hosted his own television program and occasionally starred in movies.

In the 1990s, Johnny continued to write and perform all types of music, ranging from gospel to pop standards to rock. He recorded songs with U2 and Tom Petty and the Heartbreakers, as well as duets with June and his daughter, singer/songwriter Rosanne Cash. His cover of the Nine Inch Nails song "Hurt" became a huge hit in 2003. In September of that year, Cash died, four months after June's death.

Johnny Cash's unique voice and simple but striking songs influenced and won over a whole new generation of music lovers, including alternative music and hip-hop stars and their fans. Cash's melting pot of American musical styles embodies the sound called country & western music.

The text of this book is set in Egyptian.

The paintings are mixed media/masonite in vintage frames.

Design: B Middleworth, Bats4bones design inc.

Library of Congress Cataloging-in-Publication Data

George-Warren, Holly. Honky-tonk heroes and hillbilly angels : the pioneers of country &

western music / words by Holly George-Warren ; pictures by Laura Levine.

p. cm.

Summary: Profiles important and influential performers of country and

western music, including the Carter Family, Roy Acuff, Gene Autry, Bill

Monroe, Patsy Cline, and Loretta Lynn.

ISBN 0-618-19100-3 (hardcover)

1. Country musicians—Biography—Juvenile literature. [1. Country music. 2. Musicians.]  I. Levine, Laura, 1958- ill. II. Title.

ML3929.G458 2004

781.642'092'2—dc21

ISBN-13:978-0618-19100-0

Special thanks to Robert K. Oermann and Michael Ochs Archives.

Printed in Singapore

TWP 10 9 8 7 6 5 4 3 2 1